T0108148

SUPER ALEC'S

VERY SUPER DAY

an adoption story

DEIRDRE KLEIN OCHIPINTI

ILLUSTRATED BY PENNY WEBER

To my miracle babies, Alec and Kate.
You have made my life complete.

Cover and book design by Looseleaf Editorial & Production, LLC

978-1-7335462-7-0

Printed in the United States of America
Published by KiCam Projects
www.KiCamProjects.com

This is Alec. He is four years old. And guess what else?

Alec was born SUPER. You know, SUPER . . .
like a SUPERHERO!

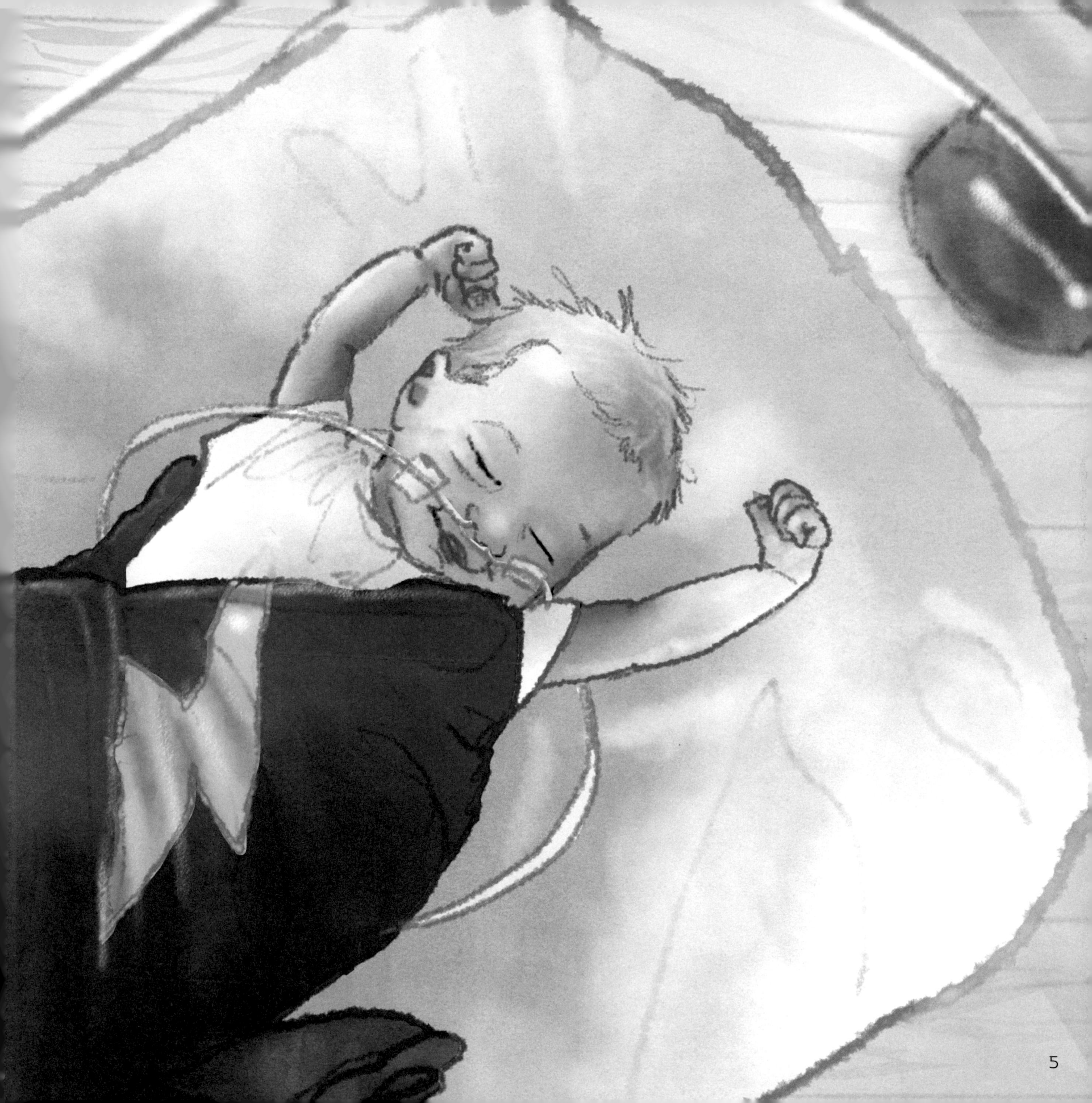

Like a lot of other
superheroes,

Alec was adopted!

Now, Super Alec lives in a cozy blue house with his mom and dad and his super dog, Snooper.

Super Alec has lots of superpowers,
and so does Snooper!

They go on lots of adventures together.

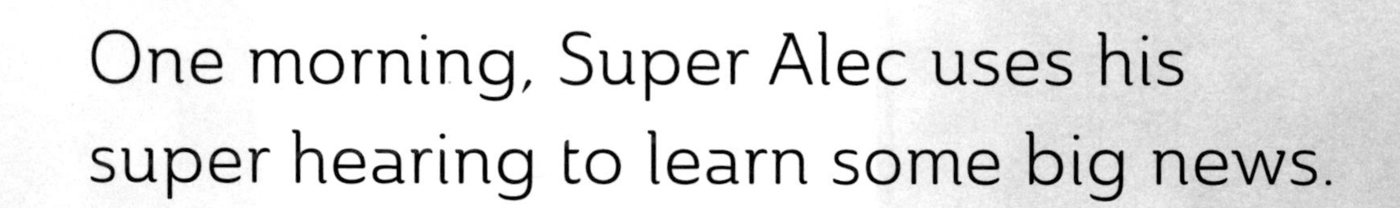

One morning, Super Alec uses his
super hearing to learn some big news.

SOMETHING VERY SPECIAL
IS HAPPENING TOMORROW!

Super Alec will need to use all
of his superpowers to get ready.

First, Super Alec uses his super mind to draw colorful pictures.

Next, Super Alec uses his super flying power to tape the pictures high up on the walls.

Then, Super Alec and Snooper move lots of stuffed animals. Super Alec has the power to talk to dogs!

And now to move that little bed with rails . . .

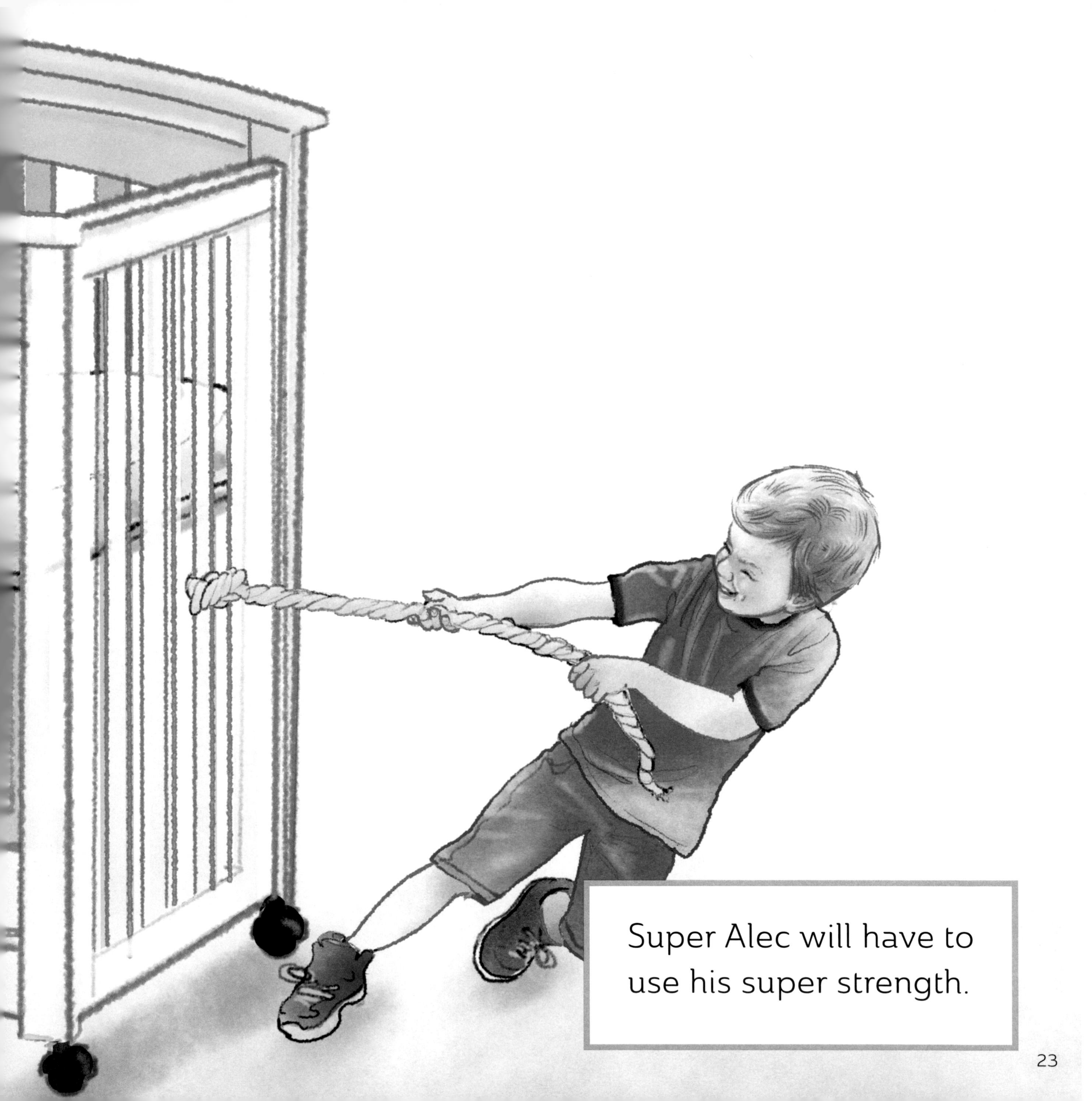

Super Alec will have to use his super strength.

After that, Super Alec goes to the back yard to make sure it is safe.

Yikes!
A snake!
Good thing Super Snooper
is there to chase it away.

Finally, Super Alec goes back to his room.
He is super ready for the special day tomorrow.

But his room is a mess!

He uses his super speed
to clean it up in a flash.

Uh oh! Bath time!

Super Alec uses his super-invisibility power to hide.

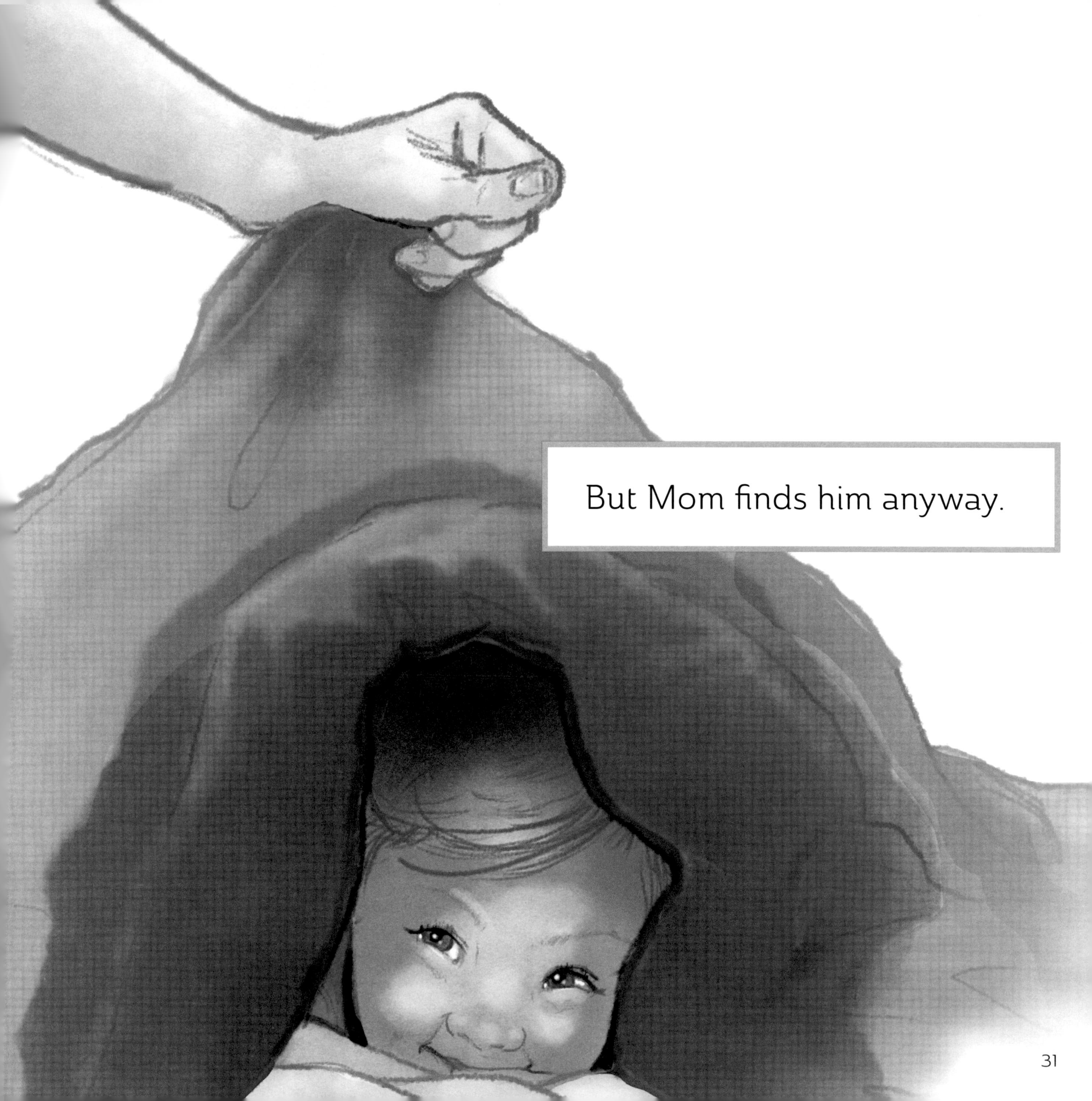

But Mom finds him anyway.

It's bedtime.
Even superheroes need their sleep.

Tonight, Dad reads a story about one of Super Alec's favorite superheroes, who was adopted just like he was!

The next morning, Super Alec
wakes up super early.

TODAY IS THE SPECIAL DAY . . .

THE DAY HIS BABY SISTER COMES HOME!

Like Super Alec,
his baby sister
is adopted.

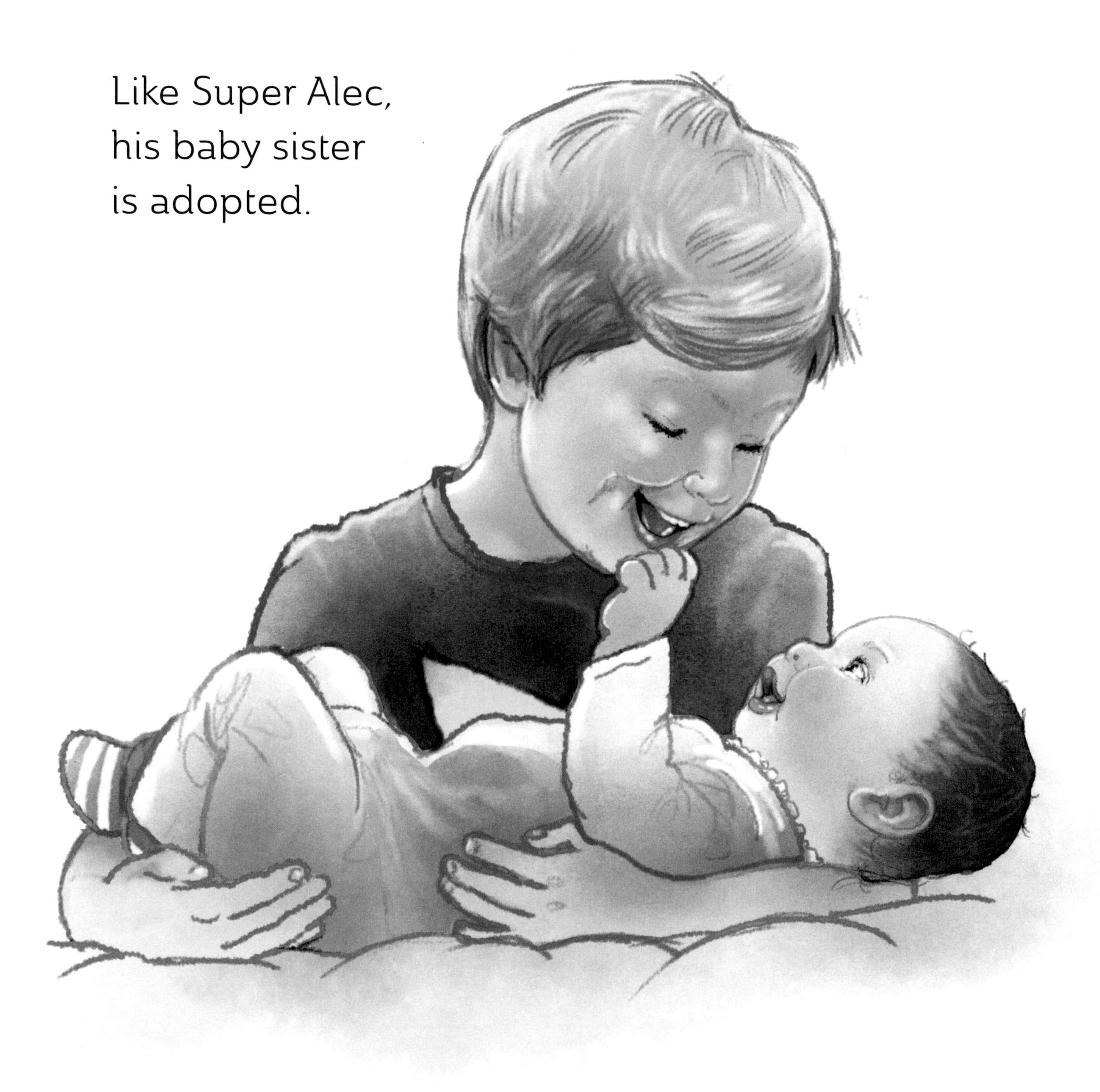

Baby Kate has superpowers too!
She uses her super-cute power to make
Super Alec smile and laugh.

Author's Note

Super Alec's Very Super Day: An Adoption Story is a unique children's book based on the true story of a boy named Alec, born into this world destined to become the adopted, beloved son of Deirdre and Joe Ochipinti (and later a brother and mentor to his adopted sister, Kate Alexandra). The story is for very young children, even newborn babies, with their happy new parents reading to them. That is when we are told to talk to our babies about adoption: at their first diaper change.

When Alec was 18 months old, I set out to find a beautiful children's book about adoption at my local bookstore. I wanted a light-hearted story that would capture and keep his attention at this young age. The few I found were located in the "Self-Help" section, giving them a negative feel. I set out to change this.

With the help of the amazing writers, illustrators, lawyers, and many others at The Society of Children's Book Writers and Illustrators (SCBWI), the story of Super Alec was ready!

What is unique about the story is that Alec was a fighter, born at 29 weeks. He was born to do great things, even after arriving into the world with great difficulty! There was no better way to show this uniqueness than by using a character all children can relate to: **a superhero**. And what better way to show how special it is to be adopted?

I hope parents will rest a little easier knowing this book can help get their adoption story started in the most magnificent way. I believe it captures my heart and soul and makes it easy to communicate: "YOU ARE SPECIAL, YOU ARE LOVED UNCONDITIONALLY, AND YOU ARE HERE TO DO GREAT THINGS."

Our amazing and unique family was God's plan.

> *"For I know the plans I have for you," declares the LORD, "plans to prosper you and not to harm you, plans to give you hope and a future." —Jeremiah 29:11*

To learn more about my story: www.deirdrekleinochipinti.com

Learn More About Adoption

Tens of thousands of children are in desperate need of adoption, whether it is through private organizations or state foster care. Visit any of these links to find out more about how adoption can change the lives of kids (and yours as well):

www.adopt.org
www.davethomasfoundation.org
www.adoptamericanetwork.org
www.adoptioncouncil.org
www.adoptuskids.org
www.nationaladoptionday.org
www.awaa.org